T0085819

CORNELIA MAUDE SPELMAN

A FOOT IS NOT A FISH!

FREDERATOR BOOKS

eBook 978-1-62726-136-4
Paperback 978-1-62726-137-1
Hardcover 978-1-62726-138-8

Text and illustrations by Cornelia Maude Spelman

Executive Editor and Publisher: David Wilk

Book design by Barbara Aronica-Buck

Frederator Books
www.frederatorbooks.com

www.corneliaspelman.com

Manufactured in Canada

INTRODUCTION

One of our important responsibilities as parents, grandparents, and teachers is to reinforce and support our children's perceptions of reality, and to strengthen their ability to distinguish what is real, true, and provable from what is belief or opinion or wish. They do learn, naturally, as they grow from babyhood, what is real and true; they delight in recognizing that a story or a game is "pretend," and are quick to object when someone else says something that they recognize is "not true!"

This book aims to playfully illustrate common and observable truths by making absurd comparisons: "a foot is not a fish." It aims to show that it is not hard to see what is true, and it also tries to establish that, to make sense of our mutual world, agreement about what is true is necessary. What if some of us thought that a foot was a fish?

Children understand that while different people have different beliefs and opinions—such as about religion, or what is good to eat—they also understand that beliefs and opinions are not the same as facts, such as what is "night" or "day." Reality cannot be changed by simply saying the opposite of what is true: "we can't just say that red is green."

Children also understand that there is a difference between a wish and what is true. They understand, once they are past toddlerhood, that we cannot change the truth just by wishing or hoping: "a wish is just a wish." They know that, although they might wish it to be so, every day cannot be their birthday.

Encouraging children to create their own verses (rhyming or not) can be fun, and can further help them in their understanding of what is real and what is not. They undoubtedly will come up with surprising and funny examples of their own. A_____ is not a _____!

A FOOT IS NOT A FISH,

AND A CAT IS NOT AN EGG.

CHICKENS DO NOT BARK,

AND A HAND IS NOT A LEG.

A PEACH IS NOT A PEAR,
AND A "D" IS NOT AN "E."

THINGS ARE JUST WHAT THEY ARE,
ON THAT WE MUST AGREE.

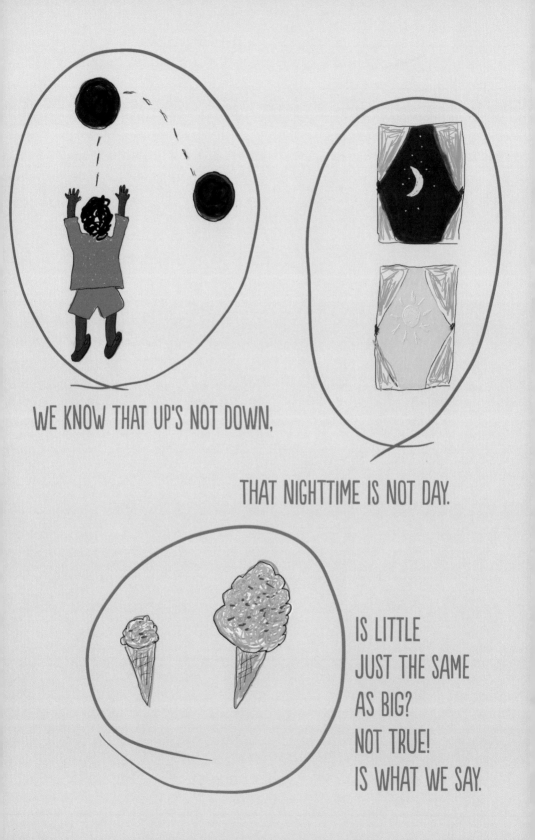

WE KNOW THAT UP'S NOT DOWN,

THAT NIGHTTIME IS NOT DAY.

IS LITTLE
JUST THE SAME
AS BIG?
NOT TRUE!
IS WHAT WE SAY.

SOMETHING REAL IS CALLED A FACT.
A FACT IS WHAT IS TRUE.

WE CAN'T JUST SAY
THAT RED IS GREEN—

OR THAT WHAT
IS OLD IS NEW.

FACT:

UP
IS
UP

FACT:

DOWN
IS
DOWN

FACT:

BIG
IS
BIG

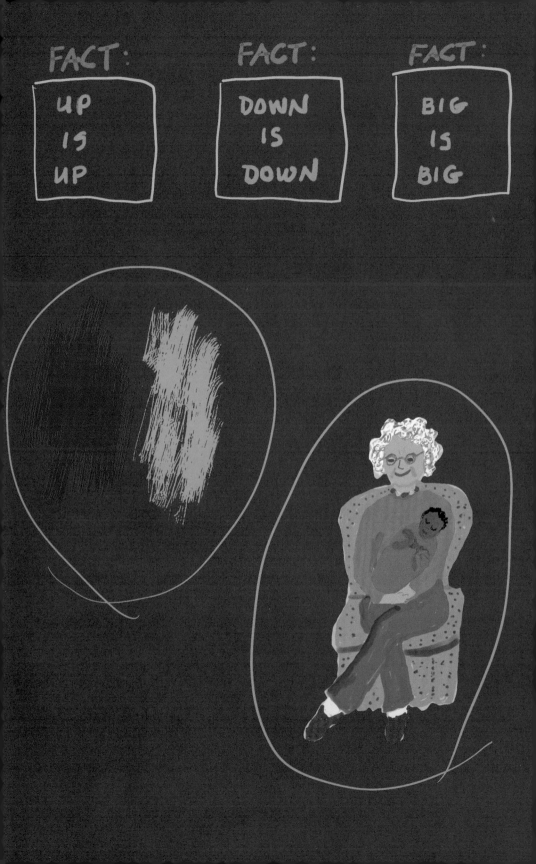

IT'S REALLY, TRULY SO
THAT TO STAY IS NOT TO GO!

IT'S POSITIVELY RIGHT
THAT THE DAY
IS NOT THE NIGHT!

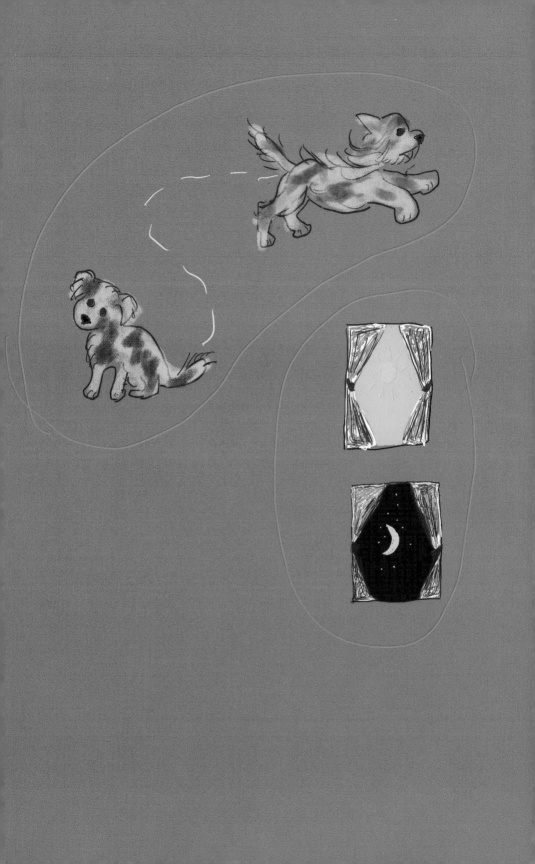

LIKE CATS AND EGGS, LIKE FEET AND FISH,
LIKE PEACHES, PEARS, AND "D,"

FACTS HAVE A WAY OF STAYING FACTS,
ON THAT WE MUST AGREE.

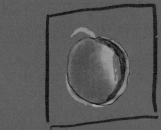

IF SOMEONE SAYS THAT UP IS DOWN
OR WHAT IS HIGH IS LOW,

THAT ELEPHANTS ARE JUST LIKE PIGS,
WE'LL SAY NOT YES, BUT NO!

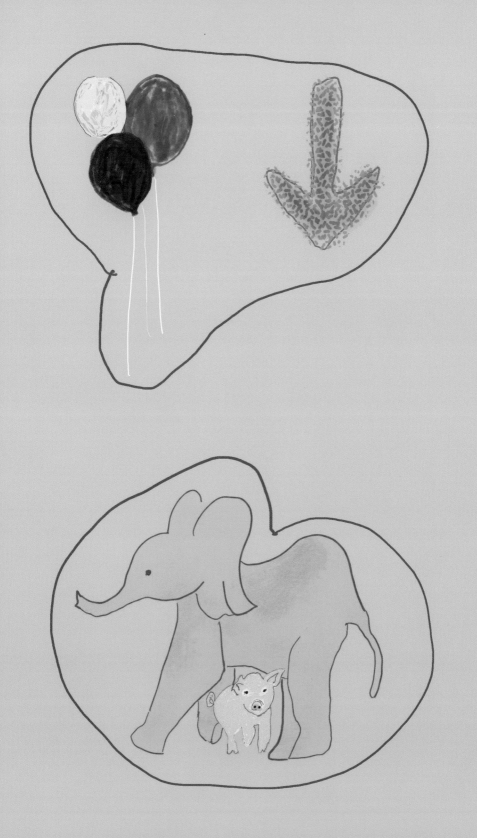

'CAUSE SAYING WHAT IS JUST NOT TRUE,
PRETENDING IT IS RIGHT,
IS JUST LIKE SAYING DOWN IS UP
OR DAYTIME IS THE NIGHT.

WE NEED TO KNOW JUST WHAT IS TRUE,
TO KNOW WHAT'S REAL, WHAT'S NOT,

'CAUSE IF WE GET THEM ALL MIXED UP,
WE'LL BE CONFUSED A LOT!

EVIDENCE IS WHAT WE NEED,
REAL THINGS THAT WE CAN SEE.
WHEN PEOPLE GET THE FACTS MIXED UP,
WELL, HOW CAN WE AGREE?

EVIDENCE IS CALLED "THE FACTS."
A FACT IS SOMETHING TRUE—

LIKE, I AM ME AND YOU ARE YOU
AND ORANGE IS NOT BLUE.

A WISH IS NOT A FACT,
A WISH IS JUST A WISH.
I'D LIKE MY BIRTHDAY EVERY DAY,
BUT A FOOT IS NOT A FISH.

IT'S REALLY GOOD TO KNOW WHAT'S TRUE,
WHAT'S TRUE AND NOT A WISH,
OR ELSE WE MIGHT GET ALL MIXED UP,
AND CALL A FOOT A FISH!

Books pack a magic all their own!

There's nothing quite like the magic a great book creates, one that you'll love to read over and over again.

We love books.

We created Frederator Books to help keep alive the special magic of books in the digital age. We've chosen great characters, artists, writers and stories to deliver the timeless wonder of words and pictures for you to enjoy with the same pleasure we had in creating them.

Together we and our creative team hope you will cherish these books as much as we do.

Visit us at frederatorbooks.com. Let us know how we're doing.